Chosen Vessel

Many Are Called But Few....

SAMUEL MCGILL III, Th.B.

Published by Word Therapy Publishing
August 30, 2017

ISBN-13: 978-09755163-3-1

Cover Design by: SharperFX, Atlanta, GA

Word Therapy Publishing
P.O. Box 939
Hope Mills, NC 28348

www.wordtherapypublishing.com

DEDICATION

This book is dedicated to

<u>My Daughters</u>:
Alexus S. McGill
Adaysha M. McGill
and
Derrick Trevon Watts-McGill
(My Deceased Son)

Also to Augustine McGill, Mattie C. Simmons and Martha Thirkield. My mother, my grandmother and my aunt. There would not be a Bishop Samuel McGill III without the contribution that these women made in my life. Each had their role and responsibility but the sum total of who I am is because of what each gave to me. I will forever love each of them. May they rest in peace.

ENDORSEMENTS

I want to commend Samuel McGill III for his tenacity through tragedy. He has what I call "the bounce back factor"! As you read the riveting pages of this, his second book, *Chosen Vessel,* I am sure that you will agree with me that it was well worth the investment in yourself as well as your future.

Many are the afflictions of the righteous, but The Lord delivers us out of them all. If we can keep that in our mind, we would indeed go further. I recommend *Chosen Vessel*, it is a good read. It is simplistic, and it will leave you encouraged to know that if he endured, that you can endure as well.

I am confidant after reading this book that each of us will have an unequivocal yes to pursuing our purpose in Christ, and will follow Him even more closely, as we accept that we are indeed all Chosen Vessels!

Bishop Donald Hilliard, Jr., D. Min.
Senior Pastor, Cathedral International
Perth Amboy, New Jersey

"*Chosen Vessel*" by Bishop Samuel McGill III is Anointed, Blessed and Scripturally sound! This God-inspired work is a 'must read' for All Believers of every age and Denomination. "*Chosen Vessel*" is a life-changing, groundbreaking masterpiece that I wholeheartedly, highly endorse and recommend!

Gary Hines, Sounds of Blackness
Grammy Award Winning Recording Group

Bishop Samuel McGill's book presents relevant and mind elevating information, which leaves readers with a fueling sense of encouragement regarding being chosen by God Himself. Not only does he highlight the importance of being chosen, but reminds us that we must in fact partner with God on our earthly Kingdom assignment in order to be truly successful as we journey through life. This book is a must read and is sure to bless all who read it!

Evangelist Lynette David
Lynette David Ministries
Columbus, Ohio

Bishop McGill, thank you for listening to God and blessing the people of God through writing, "The Journey of Life and *"Chosen Vessel"*. I was inspired by your willingness to share your experience and then to encourage others to fulfill their purpose. I recommend everyone read and receive the message of God "for such a time as this". I pray God's continual blessings on you and all your endeavors in the future.

Pastor Deidre Carter
Senior Pastor, I Walk By Faith Ministry
Gonzales, Louisiana

Bishop Samuel McGill's *"Chosen Vessel"* highlights the myriad treasures of being divinely CHOSEN by God despite ethnicity, socio-economic status, education, or pedigree. McGill uses his personal journey and discovery of Spiritual Truths to inspire readers to discover and embrace the liberty of operating in their authenticity!

Cassandra Cleveland-Robertson
National Gospel Recording Artist

Bishop Samuel McGill III's *"Chosen Vessel"* is a must read for those who are seeking to understand how to embrace the plan that God has for ones life and equip them with the tools necessary to face the obstacles that comes to frustrate and hinder God's divine plan. You will be inspired and encouraged. Bishop Samuel McGill is one of the worlds leading prolific and profound voices today around the globe and an inspiration to many.

Dr. Pauline Key-Plummer
Ambassador, President's Volunteer Service Award

Bishop McGill writes another end time message that inspires individuals not to settle for less but the greater. This literary work will refresh your mind, body and soul. He provides the tools, which will shift you from despair to the cutting edge of greatness. The words in each chapter reveals the truth behind the story, but motivates you to leap into another realm of being chosen for the task and assignment God has tailor made for your life's destiny.

Kimani H. Davis
CEO, Transform Agency, LLC.

FOREWORD

Chosen Vessel means to Julius and I that we (God's Chosen) were not a mistake and that God has a plan for all of our lives if we allow the space for his presence in us.

Then we can choose to live a life bigger than ourselves and Bishop McGill is proof that God's plan for our lives is something to strive for.

Viola Davis & Julius Tennon
JuVee Productions

ACKNOWLEDGEMENTS

First I must give honor to God for without him I can do nothing.

To Alexus S. McGill and Adaysha M. McGill my two daughters who absolutely have been a source of strength in my life and have helped me to be able to make it on this journey called "Life."

To Florida State Representative Kimberly Daniels thank you for being a true friend and my sister in the Lord. Remember I'm a Peter...LOL

To Elder Lisa Austin Granville of Woman With A Sword Ministries thanks for being a true friend. What an awesome job you are doing in the Kingdom. The best is yet to come for you and your ministry.

To the Honorable Bishop Charles H. Ellis, III love you sir and the AGAPE Fellowship of Pastors.

To Bishop Willie Martin, Jr., Elder Ivan Elam and Ronnie Timmons who are true friends and men of God that I love and respect very highly. Thanks for being the fulfillment of scripture, "A Friend Loves at All Times!!"

To Toni Henderson-Mayers and the entire staff of Word Therapy Publishing who pushed my to get this body of work out. I appreciate you all so much.

To my brother Mario A. McGill I am proud of you man. Always remember this, "At the end of the day, You're a Man of God!!"

To the Pastors of All Nations Fellowship of Churches. I am proud to serve as your Presiding Bishop.

To Stellar Award Winning All Nations Radio and the All Nations Riders who are truly ride and die. You all are some of the most amazing people. Thanks for allowing me to encourage you and speak into your lives. You guys ROCK!!!

TABLE OF CONTENTS

Chapter One

Before Your Were Born

Often times we do not understand the power of realizing that we were created before the foundations of the world. I know it's mind blowing when you really take the time to think about it. Understand this and hear me good, you were created in HIM (God) before the foundation of the world was laid in existence.

He already had a plan for your life. We can find additional confirmation of this in Jeremiah chapter one verse five where it says, "Before I formed thee in the belly I knew thee; and before thou camest forth out of the womb I sanctified thee, and I ordained thee a prophet unto the nations.

As you read this book look back over your life and I believe you will be able to say in some way that truly the hand of the Lord has been on your life. Well the point I want to drive home is it didn't just get there at the point of your remembrance it was there BEFORE!!

That's right before your parents went to lover's lane and conceived you God already knew you by name and all this was done before you were born! No matter what life does to you or even where you may be now you have got to really receive the fact that you were predestined by God for greatness.

Predestined is a powerful word. Look at it real close the prefix is "Pre" simply means before and the root word "Destined" means destination. Hmm seems like God is trying to tell us something that we really catch and that is he had already know our destination before.

I know that is kind of difficult to comprehend fully but hey he is a Sovereign God that is able to do exceedingly and abundantly above all that we could ever ask or think. You just didn't stumble up on being anointed and appointed. It was no accident. It was the Will of God.

That's why you have to be so careful what you allow to be spoken over your children even while they are in the womb even what we name our children. I know it was no mistake that I am named Samuel. Which in the Hebrew means asked of God.

Some may ask well how did God choose me before I was born? Are you ready for the answer? Well here it is simply because it was his prerogative. Remember many are called but few are chosen. The difference is we answered the call.

Journal Moment

_____

_____

_____

_____

_____

_____

_____

_____

_____

_____

Chapter Two

Growing Up In A Hard Environment

Mobile, Alabama becomes now the canvas by which I begin to paint the picture of my journey. Life has a funny way of throwing things at you. I grew up in an area that was called "The Campground." I can't remember our house number but it was on Basil Street and I also have a very faint recollection of things growing up there in terms of family activity but I do remember the candy lady that lived at the end of the street.

What was so cool about living on Basil Street was the fact that our grandmother lived right around the corner. Now I do remember that address because that's where we were most of the time and that was at 254 North Pine Street. What is so amazing is that the same house I pretty much grew up in is still there. Also Mrs. Ernestine who was our next-door neighbor who use to bath me as a little boy her house is still standing also.

Whenever I get a chance to go to Mobile and drive by there it brings back so many memories of growing up in a hard environment.

This area was known for prostitution, drug use and gangs. It was to the point that you better not get caught coming across Davis Avenue after dark. And you really didn't play to far from your front door.

Times were hard then not only growing up there in the campground but how we grew up period. I can remember our grandmother taking us to a store named National or Big "D" as we called it and you could literally buy tennis shoes in the grocery store. They were on the shelves just like the cereal and as a kid in that area you felt good to go to the store and to be able to buy a pair of shoes even though you knew you were going to be made fun of because they were no name or Bo Bo's is what they used to call them.

You could hear gunshots ring out at night and would most certainly have to lock your doors and put the extra sliding lock on as well. I can see that green shotgun house now even as I am writing. Basically one front door and all the way at the other end of the house is the back door.

I can remember sometimes even having to eat cereal with water because there was no milk or if there was milk it was the powered welfare milk that made water taste better. Eating grilled cheese sandwiches made with government cheese that was so hard that it took hours just to melt it. On the TV there were just whatever channels you could get with rabbit ears with aluminum foil on the ends to try to help with reception.

What I can say now looking back is that even though we were in a hard environment I was able by the grace of God not to become a product of my environment when so many others were and I can only attribute that to my grandmother Mattie C. Simmons. She literally made us go to church, which of course was right in the center of the projects.

Most of us to be honest with you have come up in some hard environments. I know for me it was almost like being in a prison sometimes because you always had to be watching over your shoulder. I remember one time when we were at my grandmother's house and a man had came to the door and said his car had broke down and then later that night when my grandmother was gone to church Mr. Buddy who lived in the other room in the house must have opened the door to this same guy who must have came back.

We were in the one room that my grandmother and the rest of us stayed in and heard a scuffle and then a loud noise came to the door and my cousin opened it and the man was robbing us but didn't even see my grandmother's purse hanging on the door with money in it.

Eventually he left and when my grandmother got home we called my Uncle Sidney and he came with his shotgun. Well come to find out in the next room the noise we heard was Mr. Buddy being murdered. The man who came back to rob us actually killed Mr. Buddy it was only God that we didn't get killed as well. In the room with me was my cousin and sister because we stayed home while our grandmother had went to church.

Growing up in a hard environment was just that hard! Just thinking about that night from then on knowing a man right in the next room was stabbed to death was mentally torturing because you didn't know if it would happen again. I can even now here everybody crying and seeing the police lights shining down our street. Man it was hard growing up in the campground.

Well remember I said you better not get caught coming across Davis Avenue after dark well one night I did. I was trying to make it back to my grandmother's house coming from the projects I had crossed Davis Avenue and out of no where someone grabbed my neck and snatched the gold chain I had on. Now I must note that this was no big expensive chain. It was a chain that I had got from Spencer Gifts.

I believe I ordered it from the Spencer Gifts magazine. Well I was not successful in stopping what was happening to me and ran home or to my grandmother's telling my sisters what had happened to me. If you grew up in a hard environment I know this is probably having you to go down memory lane and probably is reminding you of some of the things you had to experience in your own journey.

What I can look back and be thankful of is that even though I grew up in a hard environment God didn't allow my to be a by product of my circumstance or what was going on around us. Some people's environments and circumstances affect many adversely but if I could share anything with you from mine it would be God has a plan for you.

I say God has a plan for you because even now looking back nothing comes to mind of me making it through and out of my environment but God. I remember a time when my mother and her friend had began to so drugs and there were needles all over the place and I was in the back and wanted to go to my Grandmother's house and they wouldn't let me. I cried and was so angry that I remember biting my hand because I was so mad and didn't want to be there with them doing what they were doing.

This was so hard to deal with as a child. I know that it was a result of hurt she must have had inside her from losing my father, which I will talk about later. Not everyone is born and raised in an environment of opulence some have journey's like mine and even yours. What I feel is important to know is you can be different in spite of your environment.

I can remember times where my mother would be beaten and jumped on by different men and what is so painful is I remember one time she was beaten so badly that her jaw was wired shut. You talk about a hard environment man this is certainly one. My hope is that my experience and journey will help you as you are on your journey of life and that it would provide a sense of encouragement and motivation for you.

Syrup sandwiches and buttered toast with sugar sprinkled on it was a normal thing. Wow, as I reminisce I kind of laugh even though it was not funny then. You just look back and realize how far God has brought you. I guess too while you are in the environment you try your very best to make the best of it. I had a friend tell me that oatmeal is better than no meal. The point is something is better than nothing so truly in the end we can't complain.

I want you to receive this whether you have just come out of a hard environment or still in it as you read this book, know this that there is something so special about you that your situation can not take the fire out of your heart. What I am trying to say is I believe you will be able to make lemonade. You will take all that your hard environment is throwing at you, the sour and bitter and make lemonade out of it all.

Many have heard the saying, "You will not live to see eighteen." Well guess what? I am well pass eighteen. Growing up in Mobile was hard but I guess I was harder because I made it out and so can you. Now your hard environment may not be a city. It may be a relationship. It may be mentally but whatever it is you will not be a by-product of your environment.

I have to as they say, "Keep it Real" because sometimes I think people are ashamed of where they have had to come from and what they have had to endure. Wow, what just popped in my mind is, "It aint where you from it is where you at!" I know that may not be grammatically correct but nonetheless it is true. Keep pushing through your hard place.

Take everything that you have had to experience or may be experiencing now and use that as the fuel that allows you to keep traveling down the road of life because remember after all it is a journey.

Journal Moment

_____

_____

_____

_____

_____

_____

_____

_____

_____

Chapter Three

Young Samuel

Inside every king there is a kid who really was a king already and just didn't know it. I want to introduce you to Young Samuel. We never know what we will be especially since one can't really understand the awesome privilege of being used by God.

It kind of strange because I can't remember a whole lot about my childhood. I sort of remember patches here and there but nonetheless I want you to know the kid that was a king then and didn't know it.

Now I must show you that God really does have a sense of humor. As a young kid I was the comedian of the family. I kept everybody laughing all the time. I would make fun of preachers and the way they would, "HACK" when they preached.

Well guess what God got the last laugh. How you may ask? Simple, I ended up being a preacher myself. Now isn't that funny…LOL

Thank God for Mattie C. Simmons because she was training us up in the way we should go. She would make us read the model pray as found in Matthew 6:9-13, "After this manner therefore pray ye: Our Father which art in heaven, Hallowed be thy name. Thy kingdom come. Thy will be done in earth, as it is in heaven. Give us this day our daily bread. And forgive us our debts, as we forgive our debtors. And lead us not into temptation, but deliver us from evil: For thine is the kingdom, and the power, and the glory, forever. Amen.

The model prayer wow I remember that it was made out of foam and we had to read from it each night and then she begin to make us memorize it and recite it. Mattie C. Simons wasn't anything to be played with she meant Jesus all the way.

My grandmother looking back played a big part in shaping me into the Man of God that I am now. I can remember her locking us out of the house if we didn't want to go to church. Her motto was if you are not going to church you're not staying in the house.

I know it seems funny but it worked because when it got cold I was like I am going to church because I refused to freeze. So yes now Young is now going to church.

I remember going to Nazaree Baptist Church and being a part if the Sunbeam and Crusaders. So looking back I can remember going to church with my grandmother all the time and I do mean all the time. The mothers of the church use to call me little Samuel or little Sammy.

My grandmother to this day has a rich legacy in that church. There's no way you can mention Nazaree Baptist Church and not mention two names, Reverend Joseph Blair and Sis. Mattie C. Simmons.

The big part to summer was Vacation Bible School. I loved getting the punch and cookies (LOL). Young Samuel was being shaped by God and didn't even know it. I remember sitting in church and my grandmother would be in the choir stand and I would whisper to her asking if I could come sit in the choir stand with her.

Once I got to the choir stand with her I would lay my head in her bosom. Again Young Samuel was being made and molded and I didn't even have a clue on what God was doing in me.

I can remember even today seeing my grandmother march around the offering plate. What is so funny even thinking about it now is my brother and I would mimic her marching around the offering plate with her shawl. She was so on fire for God.

When it came to praising God my grandmother would not let anything stop her. I mean literally she wouldn't let anything stop her. When the spirit hit her she would take off running around the church. The ushers would try to catch her but Mattie was radical and gave God her all. I know that this mindset was being imparted in me even as a young child.

I remember this being told to me that I got baptized there in Nazaree Baptist Church but I couldn't remember that but I do remember my sister telling me she shouting, "There go Pookie!" which is my nickname. Yes it's out there now all of you know my nickname (Oh Lord). It was years later as a grown man that I got baptized in Jesus name.

It's truly amazing how much is poured into you without you seemingly knowing it just is. The old saying goes that children are like sponges soaking everything in. The church if I didn't tell you was right in the middle of the projects.

Eventually God brought me full circle back to Nazaree Baptist Church and as a preacher that had been now preaching across the country I had the opportunity on a few occasions to have preached at the same church that I was going to as a kid. Young Samuel the kid who was a king in the inside and didn't know it.

Journal Moment

_____

_____

_____

_____

_____

_____

_____

_____

_____

_____

Chapter Four

Close Encounters With Death

In case you didn't know when you are chosen of God the enemy of your soul which is Satan doesn't want that anointing and mantle to be realized and brought forth so he will try to do whatever he can to destroy it even trying to take your life.

I have had some close encounters with death but my testimony remains the same and that is, "The devil can't killed what God said shall live." Psalm 118:17 says, "I shall not die, but live, and declare the works of the Lord."

I can remember being told as a kid that there was a pot of boiling water on the stove. Hotdogs were being prepared and we know that water reaching its boiling point at 100 degrees Celsius or 212 degrees Fahrenheit or as we say in the hood scalding hot water.

Well here I am as a small kid standing by the stove and my cousin tries to peak into the pot and knocks it over on my shoulder causing sever third degree burns. I know you might have cringed just then but I still have the burn scar on my shoulder even now. Close encounter. It kind of remind me of how the devil wanted to cut Jesus off before he came into who he would be. Now I am not saying or trying to imply that my cousin did that on purpose I am saying that when you have purpose even an accident can try to snuff out your purpose.

Remember always, "I shall not die, but live, and declare the works of the Lord." Tell yourself that everyday because you are chosen vessel of God. I mean absolutely hand selected. Here's another close encounter. I was coming back from Okinawa, Japan and had returned back to the United States and went to see a friend whose ex-boyfriend didn't want to accept the fact that he was an ex.

So as I am in the shotgun house sitting in the front room. It was called the front room because you literally walked in the front door and right into this room. The back door of course was on the other end of the house straight back.

Hence they called these kinds of houses shotgun because you could stand at the front door and shoot a shotgun and it would go straight through the house. So here I am sitting on the arm of the couch in the front room and in comes the ex-boyfriend with a 9MM handgun and points it right at me and I do mean right at me. He literally places the muzzle of the gun to my forehead. You talk about a close encounter with death well here it is right in your face.

Can you imagine this with nowhere to go? The way out is being blocked and you have a gun to your head. How I got out the front door I don't remember but I did get out and into my sisters car because remember I was fresh back to the States from Japan. I tried to start the car and of course the car decides that it doesn't want to crank.

All of a sudden I hear a loud crack on the driver side window. He has now taken the butt of the gun and tries to burst out the window. When the attempt to do so was unsuccessful he begins to off load. I know some of you are saying what is he talking about saying, "Off Load?"

He begins to shoot at the car. Pow, pow, pow, pow yes multiple shots at least eight to ten shots with me still inside the car. My goodness the car finally starts up and I speed off on rims yes I said on rims because all the tires where shot out. SO I am speeding down the street with sparks flying off the rims.

I have had some close encounters with death but my testimony remains the same and that is, "The devil can't killed what God said shall live." Psalm 118:17 says, "I shall not die, but live, and declare the works of the Lord."

Thinking about it now I must be a valuable tool for the Kingdom of our God because Satan tried to get me before I came into the knowledge of what God had prepared for me to do. I remember prior to getting saved I use to party and club all the time. I was in the Marines and would go to the Enlisted Club and also club out in town.

I use to drive and didn't like riding with a lot a people so I was solo and I say this very passionately DO NOT DRINK AND DRIVE! Seeing that I was not saved and responsible at the time I did one night and as I was driving I must have blacked out behind the wheel at 70 plus miles an hour.

I was all over the shoulder of the road and hitting brick mailboxes and just tore up the car and when the car finally came to a stop the Sheriff that was trailing me said this to me, "I don't see how there is not a scratch on you and the car was messed up. Looking back it was God that protected me and protected other people as well because had he not I would have a very different story to tell probably from behind bars for vehicular manslaughter. So I pray that you now knowing my story will have you say there's no way I am going to drink and drive or it will motivate you to tell a friend or loved one not to drive and drive also.

I have had some close encounters with death but my testimony remains the same and that is, "The devil can't killed what God said shall live." Psalm 118:17 says, "I shall not die, but live, and declare the works of the Lord."

Journal Moment

_____

_____

_____

_____

_____

_____

_____

_____

_____

Chapter Five

Change of Plans

When I look back over my life I can truly say that it was the Lord that ordered my steps. I remember this so clearly I was stationed in Okinawa Japan as a U.S. Marine and as my rotation there was ending I received orders to go to California but I didn't want to go to the west coast. What is powerful about this story is that it was almost less than two weeks before we were to transition.

Why is it so powerful that there was almost less than two weeks before having to report to the next duty station? Well here it is. Trying to change orders within such a short time frame was next to impossible. There was another Marine that didn't want to go to the east coast because he lived in California that said he would switch orders with me.

When God has a change of plans for you nothing can stop it. So yes the orders right in the nick of time were changed and I ended up on the east coast. I know you can think of a plethora of things in your life that the plans shifted because of purpose and the truth of the matter is that it shifted even when I didn't know what was going on. Jeremiah 29:11 puts it like this, "For I know the plans I have for you," declares the LORD, "plans to prosper you and not to harm you, plans to give you hope and a future. Bottom line is that God simply changed my entire life because I had other plans.

Now this might make you laugh but I wanted to be a rapper or DJ. Oh and a comedian. I truly thought to myself if the rapping and DJ stuff don't work out then I was BET Comic View bound. I know its funny because God truly has a sense of humor. I certainly would have never in a million years thought that I would be one saved and number two a preacher.

If someone had told me that back then I would have told him or her that they were crazy and smoking something…LOL Well as I for stated God changed my plans. I often think of what would have happened if I had gone to the west coast. Would I be alive? Would I be a preacher? Would I have started All Nations Radio? Would I have received my President Barack Obama Lifetime Achievement Award?

Who knows if any of that would have been accomplished had I went to California at that time.

One thing I am sure of is that God saved me from something by allowing the change to happen with my orders form the Marine Corps. Know this for a certainty is that God knows what's best for our lives and will switch some things up to make sure that his will is done. Now understanding clearly that God will never make us do anything against our will. He will however present us with the opportunity to choose.

I want you to look at change differently. It has been said that people don't like change and that you can't teach an old dog new tricks and all the other saying that try to undermine change. Check out these definitions of change and maybe you will look at it in a different light. Change can be defined as the passing from one place, state, form, or phase to another: *a change of seasons.*

Wow there it is most of us can truly say that we have passed from one place to another. Come on now. We have moved from misery to ministry, from agony to destiny and of course when God has a change of plans for your life seasons change for you. I know you have had some rainy days in your life but after the April showers rain down in your life May flowers will surely spring forth.

All I can say is I thank God he changed my plans.

Journal Moment

_____

_____

_____

_____

_____

_____

_____

_____

_____

Chapter Six

The Brig

A deviation from the normal course is the definition of the word detour. Well if we are honest all of us at some point has deviated from where we were supposed to be going present company included. After the lost of my son and being stationed in Okinawa, Japan my first duty station had its affect on me.

When I got back to the States my duty station was Camp Lejeune, North Carolina where I had been for my M.O.S. School. Well I was not saved and did a lot of partying and clubbing. I carried my gun with me everywhere I went. Yes my 9MM was my best friend. I carried that gun because I thought that I looked good and was not going to tussle with anyone. I was going to shoot first and then ask questions later.

The place to be was always the Enlisted Club, City Lights Club or the Talk of the Town and I was one that hit them all. Drinking and partying was something I did on the regular. Maybe it was a way that I dealt with all of what I had faced and dealt with but I am not Dr. Phil and can't really say why I did those things back then I just did. I was just off course.

I had this white Hyundai Excel and back then it was a bad ride. I had chrome rims and a booming sound system and finally was voted in as a member of the local car club, which was Low Level Finest. Man you couldn't tell me anything.

Well like normal I would go out to the clubs but something would happen this particular night that really detoured my life in a major way. I went to the E-Club (Enlisted Club) located on Camp Geiger and yes had my gun with me. It was a little cold because I remember having on jeans and a sweater and my gun was hid underneath my sweater.

Already a little tipsy someone tried to start a fight and I pulled my gun out on him and of course a piece brings about peace. I get in my car and head off base but when I get to the front gate the MP's (Military Police) pulled me over and asked me if I had a gun and of course I lied and said no.

They searched me and found the gun loaded with 19 rounds in the clip and 1 in the chamber of the gun. Well I don't have to tell you what happened next. Yes, they immediately arrested me.

The charges piled up on me and I ended up being court martialed. A special court martial is what they gave me.

Regardless of the offenses involved, a special court-martial sentence is limited to no more than forfeiture of two-thirds basic pay per month for one year, and additionally for enlisted personnel, one year confinement (or a lesser amount if the offenses have a lower maximum), and/or a bad-conduct discharge.

So now I am in custody awaiting my trial to begin and the military prosecutor was trying to through the book at me to included the reduction in rank, forfeiture in pay and a BCD in which we called a Big Chicken Dinner or as it is really known a Bad Conduct Discharge.

A Bad Conduct Discharge would have most certainly messed me up for life. What do I do now? Well I was assigned a defense attorney and the process began. When I say the prosecutor was trying to throw everything at me including the kitchen sink that is exactly what he was trying to do.

Here is the part you really have to catch and that is my service record was impeccable. I was a pretty well decorated Marine to include

Meritorious Mast as well as Letters of Accommodations and the list goes on. Well having seen this in my records the Judge who was a Full Bird Colonel asked me, "What are you doing in my court room?"

He further said we are going to take a recess and when we come back I am handing down my sentence. Well I know this could mean loss of rank, money and being dishonorably discharged from the Marines Corps. Well still not having a bone fide relationship with the Lord I still began to pray. My prayer went like this, "Lord I don't know what you want with me but if you allow me to stay in the Marines and not be dishonorably discharged I will listen to what you have to say."

Well when the recess was over and everyone assembled back inside the courtroom. The judge said, "I'm not going to discharge you." When he said that I knew God had heard my prayer. He did however reduced me in rank, forfeiture my pay and sentence me to 120 days confinement in the Military Brig.

My life had gotten of course but God had a plan for my life and I was off to the brig.

The brig was no joke and certainly not a vacation. When I got to the intake section it was nothing I could have ever prepared for or imagined. The guards immediately called me prisoner and you could not make direct eye contact with them. All of my civilian clothes I had on at that time were taken and I was given prison orange and I don't care what no one says orange is not the new black.

Well my attitude was much different by this time. Remember I was praying at the trial Lord if you allow me to stay in the Marines I will listen to what you have to say but now I was like I am just going to do my time get out and had planned on business as usual but little did I know something was going to happen. It would forever change my life and I am so glad that it did.

Being in the brig was something totally shocking. Number one your freedom was gone. Then you had to be locked up in a squad bay dorm type setting with about 10 – 15 other prisoners (Marines). Having to shower with other men at the same time was like crazy and you best not drop your soap as they say.

You were no longer your own you had to take orders and be called prisoner and if you had a visitor they had to strip search and cavity search you which was degrading. I remember one day just putting a chit or request in the chaplain's box and asking for a Bible and when I got it I started reading it.

I mean I read it from cover to cover. I remember reading the Bible all the time. When others would play basketball for their yard time. I would read my Bible. I carried that Bible everywhere I was allowed to take it and stayed in it.

I read the entire Old Testament and then the New Testament. I remember clearly reading Acts chapter two verse thirty-eight through forty which said, "Then Peter said unto them, repent, and be baptized every one of you in the name of Jesus Christ for the remission of sins, and ye shall receive the gift of the Holy Ghost. For the promise is unto you, and to your children, and to all that are afar off, even as many as the Lord our God shall call. And with many other words did he testify and exhort, saying, save yourselves from this untoward generation."

I also remember Acts chapter one verse eight saying, "But ye shall receive power, after that the Holy Ghost is come upon you: and ye shall be witnesses unto me both in Jerusalem, and in all Judaea, and in Samaria, and unto the uttermost part of the earth." I wanted exactly what I was reading about. So I put in a chit again in the Chaplain's box but this time I was requesting to be baptized.

I said to myself if anybody come in here and try to baptize me any other way than what I read I was going to leave them in the water by themselves. Well the time came for me to be baptized and I remember these two brothers coming and there was this wooden box filled with water but only one person could fit in it and I had to curl up in the fetal position just to fit in the box. The two brothers that came were Brother Vernon Miller and Elder Larry Davidson.

They began to read from Romans chapter six and Acts chapter two like I did so I said to myself this is it. They were outside the box and took me and said, "Brother McGill upon the confession of your faith in the death, burial and resurrection of our Lord and Savior Jesus Christ we are going to baptize you in the name of Jesus Christ for the remission of your sins and you shall receive the gift of the Holy ghost for it is a promise unto you, your children and as many as are afar off as many as the Lord our God shall call as we baptize you in Jesus name."

Once they said that they took me down in the water but my foot came up because the box was so small and they said we have to take you down again because you need to be completely covered under water. And the said, "As we baptize you in Jesus name and took me down again and this time I was completely covered under the water and when I came up out of the water this time I felt different. I couldn't explain it but I knew something had happened.

After being baptized I keep reading the bible both day and night. I started reading about the Holy Ghost. I started seeing where people receive the Holy Ghost evidenced by speaking in other tongues as the Spirit gave them utterance and I said I want that! So one night when lights were out I got down on my knees by my bunk and started praying and felt something in my throat it scared me so I jumped in my bunk and went to sleep.

That same night I had a dream and in the dream it was as though I was looking down at myself in the dream like I was watching a movie. In the dream I was lying in my bunk and the ceiling opened up and flames of fire started to descend upon my body and when the flames hit my body I started in the dream speaking in tongues and I woke up. Later that day I placed yet another chit (request) to go to the chapel church service. I will never ever forget this day.

When I got to the chapel it was a man by the name of brother Steve from the UPC (United Pentecostal Church) that said if there is anyone here that wants something from God to come to the altar and might I say the church services were held in the upper room, which was on the very top floor of the brig. So I ran to the altar because I wanted the Holy Ghost like I read about in the Bible.

When I got to the altar I closed my eyes and totally blocked out everything around me and started calling on the only name that I knew and that was Jesus. As I called on Jesus something happened that would forever change my life. As I kept calling that wonderful name I could feel the same fire I saw in my dream I could feel it in my hands and it traveled down my arms, down my chest and all the way down my legs and when it hit my feet I heard this wonderful heavenly language that I had never heard before in my life.

It was the most beautiful distinct language that flowed like a mighty river. Well now the guard is tapping me on my shoulder and told me that I had been there now for thirty minutes and the service was dismissed thirty minutes ago and that I had to go back to my cell. As I began to take my first step I began to stagger as a person would who was intoxicated. Well I wasn't drunk but I was certainly filled with the Holy Ghost. I knew it and the devil did too.

As I got back to my cell the other brothers knew I had it to and I can say my life has never been the same. For someone reading this that may wonder if God is real I am a living witness to tell you that not only is Jesus real but he is the best thing that has ever happen to me.

From that moment on as I read the Bible it was so much clearer to me and it seems like revelation jumped off the pages like never before. Whenever anyone had a question about the Bible they would find me to ask me to explain it or one of the other brothers they knew were saved. This was so amazing that they would do that but every time someone had a question the Lord would give me such wisdom and clarity that it truly was amazing seeing him use me like that. Little did I know he was really preparing me for ministry even then and I had no idea really of what was happening.

Once I had received the Holy Ghost even though I was still locked up I had such a feeling of freedom that was so liberating and amazing. Truly whom the Son has made free is free indeed. At this part of my journey I may have **deviated from the normal course that I was on but truly the steps of a good man are ordered by the Lord and he delights in his way.**

Journal Moment

_____

_____

_____

_____

_____

_____

_____

_____

_____

Chapter Seven

Mess, Message For The Mess-Age

As you read this chapter read it with your internal eyes open on yourself. Let me put it like the young folk say, "Keep it 100!" You might be saying where is he going with this? Well the bottom line is that we all have had some mess or have some mess in our lives.

God told me that he would take our mess and give us a message for the mess (AGE). The age is in a mess and it is going to take those of us who are not afraid and ashamed of what we have had to experience to share our message with the world. So many people are hurting and are messed up simply because we hold back or we edit our testimonies.

The reason why so many sit on the raw, real testimony is based on what people might say or how they may look at us based upon the mess watch this that we have come out of or should I appropriately say that God has brought us out of simply because he was not going to let us die in the mess that we were in at the moment.

All of us have a story and that story is not to be undermined because there can never be a glory without a story. Seems to me that God specializes in choosing the underdog or the person that is messed up and I do mean tore up from the floor up.

Isn't it interesting how God somehow uses families with dysfunctionalities and you know some of us have families with some serious dysfunction. (Help us Jesus). Nonetheless he takes that mess turns the mess into a message and that's when we say, "Can't nobody do me like Jesus!

We aren't the only ones there are many in the Bible ordinary and normal people like us that had mess going on in their lives. Look at Jacob whose name meant heel grabber, trickster and supplanter, which means to wrongfully take the place of another. Jacob was conniving and so was his mother. My goodness if that isn't dysfunctional I don't know what is.

They both now are in cahoots to deceive the father in order to get his oldest brother's birthright. I mean they rode the whole lie out. They were partners in crime if you will. Let's peak into the text so you can see how messy this really looks.

(Genesis 27:6-30) "And Rebekah spake unto Jacob her son, saying, Behold, I heard thy father speak unto Esau thy brother, saying, Bring me venison, and make me savoury meat, that I may eat, and bless thee before the Lord before my death. Now therefore, my son, obey my voice according to that which I command thee.

Go now to the flock, and fetch me from thence two good kids of the goats; and I will make them savoury meat for thy father, such as he loveth: And thou shalt bring it to thy father, that he may eat, and that he may bless thee before his death. And Jacob said to Rebekah his mother, Behold, Esau my brother is a hairy man, and I am a smooth man: My father peradventure will feel me, and I shall seem to him as a deceiver; and I shall bring a curse upon me, and not a blessing.

And his mother said unto him, Upon me be thy curse, my son: only obey my voice, and go fetch me them. And he went, and fetched, and brought them to his mother: and his mother made savoury meat, such as his father loved. And Rebekah took goodly raiment of her eldest son Esau, which were with her in the house, and put them upon Jacob her younger son:

And she put the skins of the kids of the goats upon his hands, and upon the smooth of his neck: And she gave the savoury meat and the bread, which she had prepared, into the hand of her son Jacob.

And he came unto his father, and said, My father: and he said, Here am I; who art thou, my son? And Jacob said unto his father, I am Esau thy firstborn; I have done according as thou badest me: arise, I pray thee, sit and eat of my venison, that thy soul may bless me. And Isaac said unto his son, How is it that thou hast found it so quickly, my son? And he said, Because the Lord thy God brought it to me. And Isaac said unto Jacob, Come near, I pray thee, that I may feel thee, my son, whether thou be my very son Esau or not.

And Jacob went near unto Isaac his father; and he felt him, and said, The voice is Jacob's voice, but the hands are the hands of Esau. And he discerned him not, because his hands were hairy, as his brother Esau's hands: so he blessed him. And he said, Art thou my very son Esau? And he said, I am. And he said, Bring it near to me, and I will eat of my son's venison, that my soul may bless thee.

And he brought it near to him, and he did eat: and he brought him wine, and he drank. And his father Isaac said unto him, Come near now, and kiss me, my son.

And he came near, and kissed him: and he smelled the smell of his raiment, and blessed him, and said, See, the smell of my son is as the smell of a field which the Lord hath blessed: Therefore God give thee of the dew of heaven, and the fatness of the earth, and plenty of corn and wine:

Let people serve thee, and nations bow down to thee: be lord over thy brethren, and let thy mother's sons bow down to thee: cursed be every one that curseth thee, and blessed be he that blesseth thee.

And it came to pass, as soon as Isaac had made an end of blessing Jacob, and Jacob was yet scarce gone out from the presence of Isaac his father that Esau his brother came in from his hunting.

OMG is all I can say. Scandalous right but we all know that God used this dysfunction in the end for his Glory. If he did that with them, why do you not believe he will do the same in your situation? There are other examples in the Bible like David. Yes you know it David who is coined as one having a heart after God had mess in his life too.

Let's peak at his story in II Samuel 11:1-15, "And it came to pass, after the year was expired, at the time when kings go forth to battle, that David sent Joab, and his servants with him, and all Israel;

and they destroyed the children of Ammon, and besieged Rabbah. But David tarried still at Jerusalem.

And it came to pass in an eveningtide, that David arose from off his bed, and walked upon the roof of the king's house: and from the roof he saw a woman washing herself; and the woman was very beautiful to look upon. And David sent and enquired after the woman. And one said, Is not this Bathsheba, the daughter of Eliam, the wife of Uriah the Hittite?

And David sent messengers, and took her; and she came in unto him, and he lay with her; for she was purified from her uncleanness: and she returned unto her house. And the woman conceived, and sent and told David, and said, I am with child. And David sent to Joab, saying, Send me Uriah the Hittite.

And Joab sent Uriah to David. And when Uriah was come unto him, David demanded of him how Joab did, and how the people did, and how the war prospered. And David said to Uriah, Go down to thy house, and wash thy feet. And Uriah departed out of the king's house, and there followed him a mess of meat from the king.

But Uriah slept at the door of the king's house with all the servants of his lord, and went not down to his house. And when they had told David, saying, Uriah went not down unto his house, David said unto Uriah, Camest thou not from thy journey? Why then didst thou not go down unto thine house? And Uriah said unto David, The ark, and Israel, and Judah, abide in tents; and my lord Joab, and the servants of my lord, are encamped in the open fields; shall I then go into mine house, to eat and to drink, and to lie with my wife?

As thou livest, and as thy soul liveth, I will not do this thing. And David said to Uriah, Tarry here to day also, and to morrow I will let thee depart. So Uriah abode in Jerusalem that day, and the morrow. And when David had called him, he did eat and drink before him; and he made him drunk: and at even he went out to lie on his bed with the servants of his lord, but went not down to his house.

And it came to pass in the morning, that David wrote a letter to Joab, and sent it by the hand of Uriah. And he wrote in the letter, saying, set ye Uriah in the forefront of the hottest battle, and retire ye from him, that he may be smitten, and die.

Wow that sounds like murder in the first degree to me, but again somehow God in spite of

David and the consequences he had to pay used this mess and we read the message even now. The point I am trying to drive home is that God already factored in your mess and told me he will take our mess and give us a message for the mess-AGE!

Journal Moment

_____

_____

_____

_____

_____

_____

_____

_____

_____

_____

Chapter Eight

Prophecy Spoken

Prophecy is known as a message inspired by God, a divine revelation. The Bible says that prophets "spoke from God as they were moved by "Holy Spirit." (II Peter 1:20, 21) So a prophet is one who receives God's message and transmits it to others.

It is amazing how God who does not need to communicate with us does and loves to commune with us. Let that simmer in for a moment. The God of the universe wants to communicate with you. He does that to let us know that he has us on his heart and mind.

I know the Lord wanted me to share with you these prophetic words and utterances that God has spoken to me over the years and even recently and I wanted to share with you prophecy spoken.

This Word was given to me by a great woman of God which is Pastor Sue Jones who is already now with the Lord.

The Word of the Lord, *"I see International flags. The Lord says you've reached large things before but it's a new season in your life. Don't expect it to come for you like it has before. The Lord says ask largely of me. He is your source. Stretch out on faith. It is ordained of me saith God. What you have in "From Pain To Power-The Movement" is a last day move of God. I see God's fingerprint all over you."*

~ Pastor Sue Jones ~
Prophecy given 9-29-2008

The Word of the Lord, *"The Lord says that you are a true Man of God. You are a man of honor. You have an Apostolic Anointing on your life to train leaders."*

~ Pastor Cheryl Peeples ~
Prophecy given 11-30-2009

The Word of the Lord, *"God said you have been wrong. Some doors have been shut in your face and haven't been opened like they should have but God's got you. God is going to give you all the trinkets. You are going to have things in every fashion. You will look like what he has called you to be.*

78

There a vision you have that needs financing, God told me to prophecy finances for the vision. Do not worry about your past saith God."

~ Overseer/Prophet Joseph Brinson ~
Prophecy given 11-13-2008

The Word of the Lord, *"Be steadfast and continue to get closer to God. Don't get weary, be still and know that he is God. God is going to complete you. Don't let your spirit be cast down and don't let tour soul wander. It shall come to pass.*

Let not your heart be troubled for I am with you saith God. Your petition is already before me. Let your faith come up higher even though you may not see it. You are at a place in God where you are at a stand still. You are at a place where miracles are going to happen just stand still.

You have a giant to kill to cross over to Jordan and really don't know how close you are to crossing over. There's revival in you but you need help. God is going to connect you. You have a double portion on your life.

You shall live and not die. You will experience God's glory and you will be amazed. God says I need you to be strong in me that even if the situation looks dead you will say all is well. Your praise is like a warfare fighter. Just utter God I thank you for the miracle.

God is going to bring you into a wealthy place not only wealth as it pertains to finances but wealth in your spirit. Miracles, signs and wonders are coming out of you. You have a priestly and kingly anointing on your life. You will be full of prosperity all around you.

It is your set time and season. If I didn't allow you to be tried I could not have gotten my glory. God says you are special. He says your sacrifice is worthy unto him. You are going through because you have so many mantles on your life. God says even when you cry I hear your tears. When you cry I cry and when you hurt I hurt saith God. The gift of healing and deliverance is inside of you."

~ Prophetess Hall ~
Prophecy given 3-16-2010

The Word of the Lord, *"I see in the Spirit a Spiritual Steroid. Steroids enhance you. God is*

80

taking what he has already given and enhancing it. Something is happening in your ministry. God is anointing what you have. This is a season that he is stirring up the prophetic in your belly.

A fresh refreshing is on you. The Angel of the Lord is stirring up the waters of your soul."

~ Apostle Kimberly Daniels ~
Florida State Representative
Prophecy given 1-26-2017

Prophecy is known as a message inspired by God, a divine revelation. The Bible says that prophets "spoke from God as they were moved by "Holy Spirit." (II Peter 1:20, 21) So a prophet is one who receives God's message and transmits it to others.

Prophecy spoken and His Words will not return unto him void but they will accomplish that in which he set them forth to do!

Journal Moment

_____

_____

_____

_____

_____

_____

_____

_____

Chapter Nine

McGill Ministries Worldwide

Who would have known that I would be preaching and in ministry but hey when God calls you the best thing to do is simply say, "Yes Lord!" I am so amazed that God would want to use me to promulgate this glorious Gospel. I mean it's a privilege to preach the Good News.

So you can have an appreciation for where McGill Ministries Worldwide is today; I need to take you back to the beginning and bring you to the present. I can remember way back in the day having a double cassette recorder and closing myself in the room and opening the Bible and preaching to myself on the tape.

I would take the cassette tape and let some of the Saints that I was close to listen to it and they were like Oh my God is that you? I didn't really think anything of it but they told me you are going to preach one day. Well I was going to Shiloh Pentecostal Holiness Church.

At the time and I was over the Nursery Committee and also served at the Pastor's Aide President with a team of brothers that served the Bishop and it was my responsibility to oversee this department as well. Note I was just a brother if you will. Coming out of the brig God had poured so much revelation in me and the truth of the matter is I didn't even know how to flow in this gift and mantle because at the point I was a new convert.

Serving there in Shiloh was a blessing. I was appointed to be over prayer for the missionary department and one night we had a program and each missionary had to as they use to say back them a thought. Well we had seven minutes each to give our thought. God used me in such a powerful way that one of the licensed Evangelist of the church came up to me after church and said, "You preached now all you got to do is wait on God!"

She was basically saying God is going to use you to preach the Gospel and all I had to do was wait on his timing to manifest it. It was amazing because I remember as a missionary I would setup for the missionary department to go out into the streets and minister. Yes right on the corner of Hargett Street and Bell Fork Road in Jacksonville, North Carolina on the corner ministering the Word of God. Wow seems just like yesterday.

As I continue to grow in the Lord I began attending Christ Temple Church on the P.A. of W. (Pentecostal Assemblies of the World, Inc.) I was appointed to teach Sunday School I believe I had the age group of 8-10 year olds but I tell you God used me to really impart into their lives to the point that everyone wanted to be in my Sunday School class because during our Sunday School reviews my class would just show out and I do mean in a good way on their excitement and what they were learning and the ability to articulate what they learned was simply powerful.

From there I was ordained as a Deacon and yes you guessed right another program where all the Deacons were to give a thought. Now note I am the youngest Deacon out of them all. Well God gave me a thought (LOL) and it was, "The Nothing Like It Experience!"

This thought was simply a testimonial of how I received the Holy Ghost while I was in the Brig (Military Prison) and that there was nothing like receiving the Holy Ghost evidenced by speaking in other tongues as the Spirit of God gives the utterance.

Here is where it gets interesting. While I am up now giving my little thought my pastor at the time is behind me whispering, "Don't you preach, don't you preach."

Mind you I knew nothing about preaching at all. I just know that whatever it was that was on me was like fire shut up in my bones. Well he couldn't stop the power of God and before you knew it his son jumped on the keyboard and it was over the Holy Ghost swept through that place and tore it clean up off of basically my testimony.

Fast-forward now at the same church my pastor had one of his closest ministry colleagues come in to preach for an anniversary service and this Woman of God was so powerful she reminded me of a Black Kathryn Kuhlman. She was graceful but yet powerful. So with my eyes closed I was praying to myself and said to God, "If you have called me to preach let me know?" As soon as I said that she laid her hands on my should and said, "God said stand up, turn around and yield."

When I did that it was as though a wind blew me down to the floor and I begin to speak in tongues. The power of God was on me like I had never experienced before. I tried to get up but the Holy Ghost held me down and was doing a work in me. She then turned and looked at my pastor. Yes she looked at the same one who told me a few weeks earlier while I was given a thought don't you preach. Yes she look at him right in his eyes and said, "GOD HAS CALLED HIM TO PREACH!"

My journey in Christ took me on to being licensed at a minister, Ordained as an Elder and Installed as a Pastor and ultimately consecrated as A Bishop in the Lord's Church with Apostolic Succession.

God many years ago though gave me McGill Ministries Worldwide with a motto of "From Pain To Power" Instructing me that he was going to use me all over the world to speak life into his people letting them know that they do not have to stay in the pains of their lives but that they can go on to POWER!

All of a sudden it was like boom! God began to open up doors all over the world for me to preach. A Chosen Vessel and didn't even realize that before I was formed in my mother's womb McGill Ministries Worldwide was already ordained of God. Television, radio and magazines were calling for me and I was like my God.

The National *Praise The Lord Program* on Trinity Broadcast Network had me on. Rejoice in The Word on the Word Network called me and had me on. TCT Global Television and others had me on because God had decided without needing anyone's approval that he wanted to use me in a global fashion and I am still to this day humbled by the fact that the God of the Universe has need of me.

McGill Ministries Worldwide *"From Pain To Power"* is the Lord's doing and it is marvelous in my sight.

Journal Moment

_____

_____

_____

_____

_____

_____

_____

_____

_____

Chapter Ten

Miracles, Signs and Wonders

Mark 16:20 says, "And they went forth, and preached every where, the Lord working with them, and confirming the word with signs following. Amen." When there is pure preaching of the Gospel of Jesus Christ miracles, signs and wonders will follow.

To confirm means to approve or sanction. It also means to endorse. I bless God because my prayers were always for God to do something supernatural everywhere he sent me to minister the Gospel. I would always pray as I was brought out to the pulpit Lord unless you get up with me I don't want to stand up to this podium if your not going to move in the demonstration of your power and might.

I am so blessed and humbled to say that God has always stood up for me because I determined to sit down. What do you mean you might ask? Well if you humble yourself God will exhalt you in due season. I can remember very early in my ministry God just showing up and as the saying goes showing out!

I remember being elevated to the national evangelist and traveling all over preaching and looking back I feel like crying because who am I that God would decide to use me like he has truly over all these years. People everywhere I went received the Holy Ghost often times right as I was preaching.

I remember vividly preaching for The Church of Jesus Christ located in Washington, DC. It was their annual spring revival and I was the speaker for all five nights. One particular night as I was preaching the glory of the Lord fell and a little girl received the Holy Ghost as I was preaching and had began to walk down the center aisle speaking in tongues and as she made her way to the front of the church I stopped preaching and the pastor and I came down front where she was and she said these words, "I just say the glory of God!"

You guessed it the church went up to another dimension or praise and the anointing of the Lord intensified and people came down to be baptized in Jesus name. I had finished changing clothes and literally went to the Bishop's office to shower and change and when I came out they were still baptizing people. Over 21 souls in Jesus name and God was filling them with the Holy Ghost.

On another occasion in Birmingham, Alabama as I was preaching for Faith Temple Deliverance Center at there annual meeting and again God was always constantly confirming (approving, sanctioning and endorsing) my ministry. I remember a young teenager received the Holy Ghost as I ministered and to this day she is still saved and on fire for God and that has been well over ten plus years ago.

I want to say to you that miracle, signs and wonders can follow you and your ministry as well because God is no respect of person. You just have to understand that there is no spiritual anesthesia you can take lay down and wake up a giant in God. Make sure you fast and prayer and position yourself so that the Lord can use you and that your spirit stays ever so sensitive to the move of God and his voice.

Even overseas the Lord was not short of His promises. I was in Berlin, Germany doing a two week McGill Ministries "From Pain To Power" Crusade and oh my what a move of God. I mean demons were being cast out, people were being healed and delivered and set free.

People who used walkers started walking on their own. The worship was amazing and yes all the while I had a translator that we flowed as one individual even though they speaking in German as I was minister in English.

Always remember what God said in His word, "And they went forth, and preached every where, the Lord working with them, and confirming the word with signs following. Amen."

Mark 16:20

When there is pure preaching of the Gospel of Jesus Christ miracles, signs and wonders will follow. To confirm means to approve or sanction. It also means to endorse. Thank you God for endorsing not only McGill Ministries Worldwide but all the ministries around the world that are hold up the blood stained banner and preaching the unadulterated Word of God!

Journal Moment

_____

_____

_____

_____

_____

_____

_____

_____

_____

_____

Chapter Eleven

Chosen

Ephesians 1:1-4 says, "Paul, an apostle of Jesus Christ by the will of God, to the saints which are at Ephesus, and to the faithful in Christ Jesus: Grace be to you, and peace, from God our Father, and from the Lord Jesus Christ.

Blessed be the God and Father of our Lord Jesus Christ, who hath blessed us with all spiritual blessings in heavenly places in Christ: According as he hath *chosen* us in him before the foundation of the world, that we should be holy and without blame before him in love."

It is no accident that you are where you are right now as it pertains to your position in Christ and contrary to popular belief we didn't choose him, he chose us first. It is powerful thing to know that God's love looked beyond all our faults and saw our needs. He saw the fact that we would need a risen savior.

Think about it seriously for a moment and let it simmer in and realize that God hand selected you and not only that but he died for the choice he made. Now that's love!

Out of all the billions of people on the planet you are uniquely made so much to the point that you have your own unique fingerprints that no other person has and the very hairs on your head are numbered.

What does that have to do with anything you maybe saying to yourself? I say that it has everything to do with just how special being hand picked by God is and the fact that we should never take him choosing us for granted.

I want to switch gears a little and say that it is important the things we choose as well. That means friends, relationships etc. Even though God chose us it is important that we make a chose as well.

Joshua 24:14-15 records, "Now therefore fear the Lord, and serve him in sincerity and in truth: and put away the gods which your fathers served on the other side of the flood, and in Egypt; and serve ye the Lord. And if it seem evil unto you to serve the Lord, choose you this day whom ye will serve; whether the gods which your fathers served that were on the other side of the flood, or the gods of the Amorites, in whose land ye dwell:

but as for me and my house, we will serve the Lord.

So as you can see not only is it important who chooses you but equally important who and what you choose as well.

Never forget that chosen means to want and to desire. God wanted and desired us and told us that he would never leave us of forsake us. So when the enemy of your soul comes to say that God doesn't love you simply say, "CHOSEN!"

Journal Moment

ABOUT THE AUTHOR

Samuel McGill III

President Barack Obama Lifetime Achievement Award Recipient and also holds a Bachelor's Degree in Theology from St. Thomas Christian College and is the Presiding Bishop of All Nations Fellowship of Churches and the Establishmentarian of McGill Ministries-From Pain To Power.

Samuel McGill III is also the CEO/Program Director of Stellar Award Winning All Nations Radio and Label Executive of Seraphim Records. He is a current host of the prominent Christian Television Program "Atlanta Live" which airs in Metro Atlanta and Nationally via DirecTV and Dish Network.

Co-Host of The Christian View Television Program produced and hosted by Jackie Carpenter and is seen in approximately 78 million homes. He has made several National appearances on The Word Network, TCT Global Television and the "Praise The Lord" Program on TBN (Trinity Broadcasting Network).

Bishop McGill has appeared on the covers of Apostolic Voice Magazine, Majesty Now Magazine, Blest Magazine and Triumph Magazine. God has gifted and anointed him for this end time harvest.

He has blessed people across the U.S. and oversees with a theme message of "From Pain To Power." One thing that is consistently said about him and that is his love for God and people.

Bishop McGill has a deep and rich Apostolic Heritage and a heart for lost souls.

Order The Journey of Life-I'm Better Because of It! Today at www.mcgillministries.org

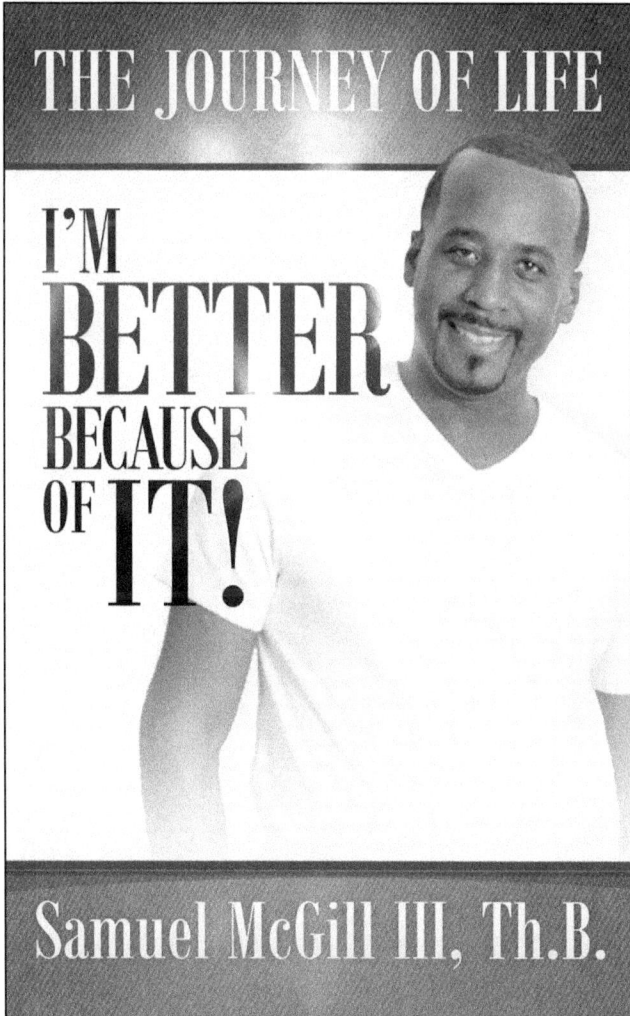

McGill Ministries, Inc.
The Worldwide Ministry of
Bishop Samuel McGill III

www.mcgillministries.org

**Tune in to the best in gospel music and
Christian programming 24/7 on Stellar
Award Winning All Nations Radio**

www.allnationsradio.net

ALL NATIONS FELLOWSHIP OF CHURCHES

2013

SERAPHIM
RECORDS

www.seraphimrecordslive.com

www.wordtherapypublishing.com

"A Message That Heals"

Tune in to our Spanish sister station with the best in Spanish gospel music and Christian programming 24/7 on Stellar Award Winning All Nations Radio

www.allnationsradionic.net